Whitney

Whitney

by Carole Portland

HOUSTON

ORION

AN ORION PAPERBACK

This is a Carlton Book

First published in Great Britain in 1994 by Orion Books Ltd,
Orion House, 5 Upper St Martin's Lane, London WC2H 9EA

A CIP catalogue record for this book is available from the British Library.

ISBN 1-85797-593-6

Edited, designed and typeset by Haldane Mason
Printed in Italy

THE AUTHOR
Carole Portland was born in San Diego, California. She is a freelance journalist and has contributed to
computer, music and film magazines.

PICTURE ACKNOWLEDGEMENTS
Photographs reproduced by kind permission of **London Features International**; **Pictorial Press** /Brett
Lee, /Mayer, /Rudi Reiner, /Giovanny Romero, /Gene Shaw, /David Seelig, /Warner Brothers, /Vinnie
Zuffante; **Redferns** /Suzi Gibbons, /Bob King, /FL Lange, /Ebet Roberts; **Relay Photos** /André Csillag.
Front cover picture: London Features International

Contents

Introduction

A the age of 30, Whitney Houston has finally discovered the really important things in her life. "Getting married and having children," she says. "It's old stuff, but it's important to me. Because how famous can you be? I've had seven consecutive Number 1 songs. What do I want? Eight? Because having all those things, having money and all that, didn't make me happy. And nobody understands that. It's always, 'Girl, to be in your shoes'. But they have no idea."

Fame has its ups—a total of ten US Number 1 hit singles and four in the UK—but it also has its downs. Whitney has been working on her career since her first manager arranged for her to skip high-school classes to attend a modelling assignment. Despite 20 years as a singer, and almost a decade in the public eye, she is constantly criticized by the press for her "lack of commitment", and dogged by allegations of temper tantrums, nepotism and (despite her marriage) homosexuality. Yet to her fans, Whitney Houston is an exquisite 5ft 10in beauty, with a voice like the purest honey, and a dignified, laudable dedication to simply making people happy.

A Star is Born

Whitney Houston seemed always destined to be a great singer. Born into a talented family, she was inspired and encouraged by them to develop her natural ability as a singer, and her family also provided the security and support she needed to become an international star.

Cissy Houston

Whitney's mother, Emily Drinkard (nicknamed Cissy), was born in 1933 in Newark. As a youngster she started singing in the family gospel group, the Drinkard Sisters, who recorded for RCA Records. The group, which featured Cissy's nieces Dionne and Dee Dee Warwick, were backing singers for several successful artists, including Wilson Pickett and Solomon Burke. Later, Cissy performed with Dionne Warwick's first group, the Gospelaires, and formed the four-piece group the Sweet Inspirations (featuring Sylvia Shemwell of Bobby & Sylvia) who were

As a child, Whitney wanted to be a teacher or a vet. "But by the age of ten…I kind of knew teaching and being a veterinarian were gonna have to wait."

*Without neglecting her
education. Whitney was
permitted to go on tour
with her mother (left).*

*Whitney with her cousin Dionne Warwick (**left**) and her mother, Cissy.*

*Like many showbusiness couples, John (**above**) and Cissy were apart a great deal. They did their best to shield their children from any problems.*

> "*Sometimes I feel like I'm really 42. I guess that's because I started so young.*"
>
> *Whitney Houston*

spotted the group and asked them to sing 'Sweet Inspiration', by Dan Penn and Spooner Oldham, which was a US Number 18 hit. They went on to record versions of 'Knock On Wood', 'To Love Somebody' and 'Unchained Melody', scoring a second hit with 'Why Am I Treated So Bad'. In the 1970s Cissy worked both as a session singer and as a solo artist. She not only released three albums (*Cissy Houston* in 1977, *Warning—Danger* in 1979 and *Step Aside For A Lady*, EMI 1980) but also worked with such varied and celebrated singers as Elvis Presley and her close friend Aretha Franklin. Remarkably she was the first singer to record 'Midnight Train To Georgia', later a big hit for Gladys Knight.

much in demand, appearing on many records from the Atlantic label between 1967 and 1970.

In 1968, after they sang backing vocals with Aretha Franklin, Atlantic Records' Jerry Wexler

Humble beginnings

John Houston was his wife's manager when Cissy was out on the road, and when their daughter, Whitney Elizabeth, was born on August 9, 1963, it was John who stayed at home to watch over her. "He was Mom's support network while she was out on tour," said Whitney, in tribute to her father. "He changed diapers, cooked, did my hair and dressed me, all the while providing Mom with advice and answers."

Together they lived in Newark, in the state of New Jersey, near New York. Although Cissy's work as a soul singer often caused her to be away from home, the family's strong religious convictions meant that they were regularly seen in the congregation at the New Hope Baptist Church, where Cissy was Minister of Music. In the natural progression of things, the church was to become the humble venue for Whitney Houston's first solo performance.

Newark

Newark in the Sixties was a place of social upheaval. In the struggle for civil rights, black people turned to the politics of the street to have their say. Anger escalated into rioting, looting and rage against the political system. As the Houston family hid in their home, John and Cissy vowed to take their children away from the city.

Although they moved to the suburban East Orange, they could not sever their spiritual link with the church, and they continued to return to the city every week. John Houston later became the Executive Secretary of the Newark Central Planning Board, and always retained his sense

"I had a song to do," said Whitney, "and then, as I got a little older, [my mother] gave me two songs to do...And I went on from there."

Aretha Franklin was one of Cissy Houston's greatest friends, and was known to the young Whitney as "Aunt Ree".

of responsibility for the restructuring of the multi-racial city.

So natural

With so much music in her parents' lives, it was only a matter of time before Whitney realized that music was in her blood: "Being around people like Aretha Franklin, Gladys Knight, Dionne Warwick and Roberta Flack, all these greats, I was taught to listen and observe. It had a great impact on me as a singer, as a performer, as a musician. Growing up around it, you just can't help it. I identified with it immediately. It was something that was so natural to me that when I started singing, it was almost like speaking."

Whitney's vocation did not strike her right away. In her infancy, she had already made up her mind to be a teacher. "I love children, so I wanted to deal with children. Then I wanted to be a veterinarian. But by the age of ten or eleven, when I opened my mouth and said, 'Oh God, what's this?' I kind of knew teaching and being a veterinarian were gonna have to wait. What's in your soul is in your soul."

Going solo

The first time Whitney's solo voice was heard in public was, naturally, at the New Hope Baptist Church. At the age of about 11 she sang 'Guide Me, O Thou Great Jehovah', and the reaction she received taught her something she would never forget. "I was scared to death," she recalled. "I was aware of people staring at me. No one moved. They seemed almost in a trance. I just stared at the clock in the centre of the church. When I finished, everyone clapped and started crying."

Dreams of stardom

Soon after, Whitney began to entertain fantasies of stardom.

In concert at Madison Square Garden: as a child, Whitney often imagined herself performing on this famous stage.

> *"God gave me a voice to sing with. And when you have that, what other gimmick is there?"*
>
> *Whitney Houston*

She would dress up in her mother's clothes, borrow her equipment and pretend to be performing on stage at Madison Square Garden in New York. "I remember when I was about 12," she said, "I would go into our basement where my mother had her recording equipment. I'd take the microphone, put on Aretha Franklin's music and go at it for hours, closing my eyes and singing all by myself. I imagined I was on stage, singing to a packed house."

It was at that age that Whitney Houston decided to become a professional singer like her mother before her. It was not just that the clamour of applause stimulated her so strongly—although that in itself was overwhelming—it was that a career as a vocalist was the only way she could imagine truly to repay God for the gift of music. "God gave me a voice to sing with," she said. "And when you have that, what other gimmick is there?"

Strict teacher

Cissy Houston has a very strong character, and her effect on her daughter's career cannot possibly be overestimated. John Houston has said that Whitney's mother taught her very strictly how to conduct herself. Cissy Houston was the product of a very traditional Baptist family. She believed in hard work and honest dedication to music, to family, and to God. Of course, Cissy's commitment to singing was far from a burden, but it is fair to say that she came from a generation of recording artists who worked really hard for their money. As a session singer, Cissy's back catalogue of recorded work is vastly greater than her daughter's. From that experience, she passed on to Whitney the priorities that had made her career so fruitful: work hard, never forget the family, and always remember that a singer's voice is a gift from God.

The essence of soul

That wonderful gift is something Whitney is never slow to acknowledge. Speaking to US magazine *Rolling Stone* in 1993 she said: "My mother was the first singer I had contact with. She sang constantly to us around the house, in church. I used to watch her, and the feeling...My mother always said to me, 'If you don't feel it, then don't mess with it, because it's a waste of time.'

"I learned a lot about voice control and how to command an audience from Dionne [below]," said Whitney. "I come from a long line of singing perfectionists, and I'm just the same way."

When I used to watch my mother sing, which was usually in church, that feeling, that soul, that *thing*—it's like electricity running through you. If you have ever been in a Baptist church or a pentecostal church, when the Holy Spirit starts to roll and people start to really feel what they're doing, it's...it's incredible. *That's* what I wanted."

Dionne Warwick

Twenty-three years her elder, Whitney's cousin Dionne Warwick was another major influence in her early years. "I learned about voice control and how to command an audience from Dionne," Whitney told the *Chicago Tribune*. "I come from a long line of singing perfectionists, and I'm just the same way."

Dionne began her career playing piano with the Drinkard Sisters, who were managed by her mother. In 1960 she formed the Gospelaires, featuring her sister Dee Dee and her cousin Cissy, and played at churches all around New York and New Jersey. The girls can be heard on records by the Drifters and Garnet Mimms and the Enchanters. In 1962

> *"When I used to watch my mother sing, which was usually in church, that feeling, that soul, that thing—it's like electricity running through you."*
>
> *Whitney Houston*

the group were spotted by songwriter Burt Bacharach, and after recording back-up vocals for the Shirelles, Dionne was signed to Scepter Records as a solo artist in 1963.

Her début single 'Don't Make Me Over' hit the US Number 21 position to become the first of more than 30 hit singles written for her by Bacharach and his partner Hal David. The most well-known of her many classic records include 'Anyone Who Had A Heart', 'Walk On By' (her first international million-seller), 'You'll Never Get To Heaven (If You Break My Heart)', 'Do You Know

*On the sleeve of the **Whitney** album, the singer gives thanks to her brothers, Gary (**right**) and Michael: "I love you. The greatest love is not only learning to love yourself, but liking who you are." It is typical of Whitney to give them credit for her achievements.*

Dionne Warwick's sister, Dee Dee, was another successful R&B performer in Whitney's talented musical family.

The Way To San Jose' and 'I Say A Little Prayer' (a million-seller in the US alone). Despite some difficult years, her career continues to flourish: in 1985 she featured on the all-star charity record 'We Are The World', which became the most successful single in US history, raising $60 million (£45 million) for African famine relief, and in 1986 she made another charity record, 'That's What Friends Are For', which became the biggest-selling US single of the year. Her sister Dee Dee had a successful singing career in her own right, and was twice nominated for a Grammy award for Best Female R&B Performance.

Family business

Whitney's two older brothers, Michael and Gary, have both helped her in her career with business and music respectively. Michael became her production manager on tour, arranging everything from the lighting hire to the catering crew, while Gary joined her as a singer, performing duets and backing vocals with his sister on stage.

It is clear that Whitney and her family have always been close, and are able to rely on each other for support. That relationship has given Whitney Houston a famously unshakeable self-confidence, which is very much a part of her personality. And as famous as she is, Whitney always seems down to earth, because her simple family background and Christian faith remind her of her ordinary roots.

Whitney with her brother—and production manager—Michael.

Strong discipline

Cissy and John sent their daughter to a Roman Catholic high school, despite being Baptists themselves. Cissy in particular approved of the school's high standard of education and its firm discipline. "Early dating, cruising around—she wasn't going to do that," Cissy said later. "She wasn't going to wear stockings until I said OK, even if her friends did. No make-up, no lipstick, no high heels. And no discussion." While Cissy was teaching Whitney to sing, she was also—even more importantly—teaching her everything a woman needed to know to be successful in the music business. Naturally, such a bitter pill could often be hard to swallow. "She didn't like it. She hated it," remembered Cissy. "Sometimes she

Whitney and her mother (left) on stage in London.

would go to her father—her brothers would, too—because they thought he was a little more lenient. But they didn't get around what I told them."

Providing her education was not neglected, Whitney was permitted to go on tour with her mother. As Cissy gained more confidence in her daughter's voice, she trained and encouraged her until Whitney was occasionally moving from the quiet anonymity of backing vocals to take the spotlight herself. "I had a song to do," said Whitney, when reminded of the early days. "And then, as I got a little older, she gave me two songs to do. And I went on from there."

TV and magazines

Throwing herself into her extra-curricular work, Whitney found a very promising career in modelling. She appeared in the US magazines *Cosmopolitan* and *Young Miss* and on the covers of *Glamor* and *Seventeen* in 1981, describing herself later as "young, kind of innocent, but sexy". Whitney's modelling career began quite by chance. "My Mom and I were in New York and a young man walked over to me and said that I should go to a modelling agency that

Whitney's modelling career began when she was spotted on the streets of New York by a talent scout.

was upstairs from where we were—that they were looking for someone like me and that I would be good. I was a little suspicious, but my Mom was

> *"Getting married and having children. It's old stuff, but it's important to me. Because how famous can you be?"*
>
> *Whitney Houston*

Whitney Houston—the successful magazine model.

with me and I said, 'What the heck, let's go see about this.' " Modelling led to offers of acting roles on television, such as the American family comedies *Silver Spoons* and *Gimme A Break*, but at the same time Whitney was in even greater demand as a singer.

As a teenager, Whitney signed up with manager Gene Harvey. "When she had just turned 18, two major labels wanted to sign her," Harvey told the *LA Times*. "But I felt it was too early. I didn't want her to have to deal with those kinds of pressures at this point." Meanwhile, Whitney's voice grew stronger and more powerful and every concert-goer who saw her perform in those early days was stunned by her teenage maturity. One of those concert-goers was Clive Davis, and he was about to make her dreams of stardom come true.

Straight to the Top

When Arista Records' president Clive Davis first spotted Whitney Houston on stage, he saw the glint of stardom in her eyes and signed her up almost on the spot, in 1983. Davis had founded Arista Records in 1975 and launched the careers of many singers and songwriters from Billy Joel to Barry Manilow. He made Whitney his own personal responsibility, and famously added a clause to her contract to ensure that if he ever moved on from Arista, Whitney would be coming with him. "He is the only head of a record company who is really involved in and knows about music," said Whitney.

Conscious of the dizzying effects of the music business lifestyle on an impressionable young woman, Davis made every effort to protect Whitney from the harsher side of the industry

Whitney's partnership with Clive Davis owes its success to their shared ambitions.

while nourishing her promising talent. By pairing the beautiful voice with the classiest and best songs and musicians, Davis knew that he would get a winning combination. Using the best minds in the business, he began laying the foundations for Whitney's career. But her fame did not arrive overnight.

Youth…and experience

The successful partnership of the star and her new boss was again largely thanks to her mother. Whitney explained it best: "My mother said: 'You know, this is very difficult but I'm going to tell you the truth: you should go where you are going to get the best out of it,' meaning, let's say a company offers you a contract and they say, 'Whitney, you can choose the songs. You can do whatever the hell you want to do.' As opposed to Arista, with Clive Davis saying: 'We'll give you this amount of money, and we'll sit down, and as far as the songs you want to do, I will help you. I will say Whitney, this song has potential. This song doesn't.' So my mother was saying to me, 'You're 18 years old. You need guidance.' Clive was the person who guided me."

With Barry Manilow, one of Clive Davis's big discoveries.

Winning team

Contrary to the opinions of Whitney's critics, the relationship worked best because Clive and Whitney both had the same goals and shared the same beliefs about entertainment. Whitney told *Rolling Stone* in 1993: "I don't like it when they [media critics] see me as this little person who doesn't know what to do with herself—like I have no idea what I want, like I'm just a puppet and Clive's got the strings. That's bullshit. That's demeaning to me, because that ain't how it is, and it never was. And never will be."

Most of all, the reason that the partnership worked so well was that Clive Davis truly believed in Whitney's talent. Soon after they began working together, they appeared on *The Merv Griffin Show* on US television and Davis explained succinctly why he thought Whitney Houston would become a star. "You either got it or you don't," he said. "She's got it."

The best and the brightest

In the early days of Whitney's professional career, she honed her craft through performance, mostly as a backing vocalist on records by Paul Jabara, gospel singer Lou Rawls, Chaka Khan, and the Neville Brothers. She also sang lead vocals for the Michael Zager Band's single 'Life's A Party'. Whitney was paired with well-established soul

Whitney once provided backing vocals for Chicago gospel singer Lou Rawls, now more famous as a voice-over artist on Budweiser commercials.

crooners like Teddy Pendergrass and Jermaine Jackson, who both released records featuring vocals by Whitney in 1984—songs that appeared on her own debut album a year later. Houston and Jackson even made a cameo appearance on American soap *As The World Turns*, mugging for the camera and singing the slushy 'Take Good Care Of My Heart'.

> *"You either got it or you don't. She's got it."*
>
> *Clive Davis*

Meanwhile, as Whitney worked ceaselessly, Clive Davis cast his net far and wide to find the best songs for her to sing, and some of the pop world's most prestigious songwriters—Michael Masser, Peter McCann, Linda Creed and Gerry Goffin—supplied the songs that would form Whitney's first collection.

Michael Masser was already a fixture in the charts, having been recruited by Berry Gordy to work at Motown Studios in 1973, where he co-wrote the Diana Ross hit 'Touch Me In The Morning'. He had been working with Gerry Goffin since 1976, resulting in the Number 1 single 'Do You Know Where You're Going To' for Diana Ross, who performed it in the hit film *Mahogany*. They also wrote the 1983 hit 'Tonight I Celebrate My Love' by Peabo Bryson and Roberta Flack.

Chaka Khan, another star for whom Whitney sang backing vocals early in her career.

Pop classics

Gerry Goffin was a songwriting institution. By the time work began on Whitney's début album in 1983, Goffin was 44 years old and had worked as a prolific songwriter for two decades. Goffin's lyrics and his wife Carole King's melodies combined to create some of the most familiar and successful pop songs in history: 'Will You Still Love Me Tomorrow?' for the Shirelles, 'Take Good Care Of My Baby' for Bobby Vee, 'Up On The Roof' for the Drifters, 'The Loco-Motion' by Little Eva and 'I'm Into Something Good', which was a UK Number 1 hit for Herman's Hermits in 1964. After Goffin and King separated in 1967, Goffin continued to write successfully with other partners. As well as writing some stunning material for Whitney Houston, Masser and Goffin wrote 'Nothing's Gonna Change My Love For You', a big hit for Glenn Madeiros in July 1988, and 'Miss You Like Crazy', which was a popular summer hit for Natalie Cole in 1989.

Linda Creed was the songwriting powerhouse behind almost all of the Stylistics' hits, including 'You Make

Whitney spent two years working up to the release of her debut album.

*"Clive Davis wasn't taking any risks," said **Rolling Stone** in their review of **Whitney Houston**. "The president of Arista invested two years and $250,000 into the making of her debut album...clearly Whitney is en route to a big career."*

Me Feel Brand New' and 'I'm Stone In Love With You' (also a hit for Johnny Mathis, in 1975). With her co-writer Thomas Bell she was responsible for a string of chart singles, most notably 'The Rubber Band Man' by the Detroit Spinners and the Diana Ross/Marvin Gaye duet 'You Are Everything'. Sadly, Linda died in April 1986, aged only 37.

Studio experts

Clive Davis did not stop his pursuit of excellence with the choice of songs for Whitney's first album, which was to be called, simply, *Whitney Houston*. It was vital that the finished recordings had the class and quality befitting soul's newest queen. So for the album's

producers Davis enlisted writer Michael Masser, George Benson's producer Kashif, and consummate all-rounder Narada Michael Walden.

Kashif had worked as a producer on a number of projects, but had been most successful as a part of Clive Davis's Arista stable of artists. His first album, *Kashif*, in 1983, was followed by *Send Me Your Love* (1984), *Condition Of The Heart* (1985) and *Love Changes* (1987).

Narada Michael Walden wrote the Stacy Lattishaw hit 'Jump To The Beat', which charted at the same time as his own single 'I Shoulda Loved Ya'. While working with Whitney Houston throughout the Eighties, Walden collaborated with several other hit-makers. 'We Don't Have To Take Our Clothes Off', which he wrote for Jermaine Stewart, was a hit in September 1986, and the trailblazing 'Licence To Kill' (sung by veteran chanteuse Gladys Knight) was the hit theme song from the 1989 James Bond film.

"Clive Davis wasn't taking any risks," said *Rolling Stone* in their review of *Whitney Houston*.

'You Give Good Love' created a small stir when US advice columnist Ann Landers criticized its "suggestive" title. Whitney showed little concern. "I don't think that the title is suggestive at all," she said. "I think Miss Landers just looked at the title and didn't hear the song itself."

"The president of Arista invested two years and $250,000 [£167,000] into the making of her début album...those pipes and those looks are not to be denied...with the right songs and settings, she could be an earth-shattering performer."

Whitney Houston—the album

Whitney's eponymous début album was released in the US on Valentine's Day 1985, and although several months passed before the young artiste was truly a hit, the success of the album was historic. When the public finally sat up and took notice, the sales of *Whitney Houston* swiftly went through the roof to the tune of 14 million. Not only was it the all-time best-selling début album in the US, it was also the most successful solo album by any black female artist. When it reached the Number 1 spot, it stayed there for 14 weeks, and held a position in the Top 40 for over a year. US magazine *People* predicted "It will take an act of congress to keep this woman from becoming a megastar."

The album really took off in 1986, to become the top-selling US album of the entire year, ahead of Madonna's *True Blue*. In Britain, where the album was released in December 1985, Whitney did not quite manage to outsell Madonna, but she did achieve the third best-selling album of the year. Unusually, a full eight of the ten songs on the album were romantic ballads, firmly setting Whitney's public image as a velvety-voiced beauty with a lovesick streak.

Whitney's early public image: a distant and elegant beauty.

'Someone For Me'

Whitney received her first mention in the British press in *Record Mirror* under the unflattering

sub-heading "Whitney Who?", in March 1985. The occasion was the low-key release of her début single, 'Someone For Me'. "The lady can sing," the feature informed us, "but only time will tell if she's really the new Aretha Franklin or Diana Ross of US press hype." In fact, 'Someone For Me' has a crashing beat and a chunky funk bass-line, but none of the fragrant charm of Whitney's ballads—it is reminiscent of great, early Prince material like 'Controversy', but is almost completely unrepresentative of her other songs.

'You Give Good Love'

The first major single release from Whitney's new album was the smooth soul ballad 'You Give Good Love'. According to Clive Davis it was selected specially to give Whitney her big break "because we wanted to establish her in the black marketplace first. Otherwise you fall between the cracks, where Top 40 won't play you and R&B won't consider you their own." Not only was 'You Give Good Love' a big R&B

"It will take an act of congress to keep this woman from becoming a megastar."

People magazine

hit in July 1985, it also made the hoped-for cross-over to the mainstream pop chart. The single spent 13 weeks on the chart, peaking at Number 3, and Whitney Houston became a pop celebrity.

A hit on video

A heart-warming, selfless love song, 'Saving All My Love For You' was the single that made Whitney Houston a household name. Written by Gerry Goffin and Michael Masser, it first appeared as an album cut by Marilyn McCoo and Billy Davis Jr in 1978. Whitney's version was the Number 8 best-selling single of the year in Britain, easily topping the charts on both sides of the Atlantic, although the record had been in the shops for quite a while before radio stations and record buyers began to catch on.

The winning gambit that clinched the record's success was the video, which gave Whitney a major breakthrough on MTV. Whitney played a sultry, streamlined "other woman", whose sugardaddy was far away with his wife and family while she waited patiently for him to return. It was a moving little tale, in which Whitney Houston looked fresh and pure, but with a very sharp edge.

Outstanding!

The following year, Whitney was presented with her first Grammy award, by her cousin Dionne

Julian Lennon looks on as Dionne Warwick presents her cousin with a Grammy Award for 'Saving All My Love For You'.

Warwick, for Best Female Pop Vocal Performance for 'Saving All My Love For You'. The national US paper *Herald Examiner* wrote "Warwick bounced up and down with obvious delight as she read Whitney Houston's name as winner." When she took the stage to accept, Whitney simply said, "Oh, my goodness. I must thank God, who makes it all possible for me!"

The evening's ceremony was televised, and the record viewing figures were estimated at 23.8% of all American households. Whitney performed the song live, and as a consequence she was presented with another award in August 1986—an Emmy for Outstanding Individual Performance in a Variety or Music Programme.

Trying to take it slow

"My Mom says that if you keep your eyes open and look around, you can learn a lot," Whitney told Steve Dale of the *Chicago Tribune* in August 1985 during her first national "warm-up" tour. "I've already seen people come and go in this business. I'm being very careful with my career, taking everything step by step. I'm in no hurry." Performing in support of headliner Jeffrey Osborne, Whitney got plenty of exposure, and although the audiences were sometimes less than enthusiastic, the critics were learning to love her.

"I always enjoy performing," said Whitney the following month, as her own tour began, "so it doesn't matter to me whether I'm the opening act or the headliner. But it will be fun to get to do a whole 60-minute show."

UK critic Nancy Culp called 'How Will I Know' "a waste of a fair voice with such a forgettable song...the last laugh will be on good old Whitney unless the rest of her material is infinitely better than this."

At around that time, with 'Saving All My Love' riding high in the charts, readers of *Rolling Stone* were sending in their votes for the end-of-year popularity poll, and it was announced in January that Whitney Houston was the readers' favourite new female singer, with 32.1% of all votes cast. Whitney may have wanted to take her career one step at a time, but her fans seemed determined to make her a superstar overnight.

'Hold Me'

'Hold Me' first surfaced in 1984 on the Teddy Pendergrass album *Love Language*. The album marked the singer's comeback, following a very severe car accident, which left him confined to a wheelchair. 'Hold Me' is a syrupy ballad dominated by Teddy's luscious, deep voice but supported well by Whitney's fresh, young sound. The single reached Number 44 in the US charts, and was finally released in the UK in January 1986, also reaching Number 44.

To hear it today, the first track on Whitney 's début album, 'How Will I Know', sounds timid and girlish. Nancy Culp, writing in UK weekly *Record Mirror*, called it "a waste of a fair voice with

Left: In April 1986 Whitney received the key to the city of Newark, New Jersey from Mayor Kenneth Gibson, watched by her proud parents.

Whitney was paired with soul crooners like Teddy Pendergrass (below) and Jermaine Jackson, who both released songs featuring Whitney on backing vocals.

Originally the 'B' side of US single 'You Give Good Love' and UK single 'Someone For Me'. 'The Greatest Love of All' did not make it to an 'A' side until a full year after the release of the album in America.

such a forgettable song", adding that "the last laugh will be on good old Whitney unless the rest of her material is infinitely better than this".

It is a bouncy, teenage song without much substance, but Whitney's fame was on such a high after the Christmas of 1985 that her voice could scarcely fail to hit. 'How Will I Know' (the only track on *Whitney Houston* to be produced by Narada Michael Walden) became her second US Number 1 and was among the top ten best-selling singles of the year in the US. In the UK, too, fans were still hot for Whitney's vocals—the single reached Number 5, her biggest hit in 1986.

A third Number 1
'The Greatest Love Of All' by Michael Masser and Linda Creed was originally written for George Benson as the theme for Muhammed Ali's 1977 biopic *The Greatest*, in which the boxer portrayed himself. At the time it reached Number 24 in the US and Number 27 in the UK.

However, in 1986 it was touched by the Whitney Houston magic. Originally it was the 'B' side of US single 'You Give Good Love' and UK single 'Someone For Me'. It didn't make it to an 'A' side until a full year after the release of the album in America, but immediately went to Number 1 in the States and Number 8 in Britain. It was even nominated as the Song of the Year at the Grammy Awards in February 1987.

World tour
Whitney's first ever world tour was a major event, with a very ambitious presentation. The star chose to perform in the round on a huge circular stage situated in the middle of each auditorium, like a boxing match, so that the entire crowd had a

clear view. The staging gave each show a dramatic yet intimate feel, and was an enormous test of her skills as a performer, as she tried to play to all "sides" at once. David Sinclair in the national UK paper *The Times* called it "a measure of her extraordinary status after only one solo album", saying that Whitney "looked like a shimmering hologram, but her command of such an intimidating area of space was real enough throughout the set".

Performing nearly all of the songs on her début album, Whitney sang a simple set to show off her vocal talent, without any costume changes. The seven-piece band was set apart from the singer, on a smaller stage below her. Whitney was alone on the stage but for a cordless microphone, although she was joined by her brother, Gary Garland, for the duets 'Hold Me' and 'Nobody Loves Me Like You Do'. The show began with Whitney singing the first few bars of 'The Greatest Love Of All' teasingly from behind a partition, before launching into the uptempo Michael Jackson hit 'Wanna Be Startin' Something' (which was one of her earliest recordings, on an Arista Records sampler LP).

Press popularity

Commenting in the *Chicago Tribune*, Daniel Brogan called Whitney "an uptown Tina Turner", saying that he could forgive her occasional ad libs and indulgences because: "It is easy to imagine just how tempting it is to cut loose when you have as much natural talent as she does." A regular highlight was the gospel standard 'I Believe' (once a hit for Frankie Laine), which David Sinclair said "swept towards the very highest of registers in waves of mounting vigour".

The tour was far more indicative of Whitney's roots than the album had been. Daniel Brogan was pleasantly surprised that Whitney seemed to be "a far bolder, far grittier performer than the MOR pop diva on *Whitney Houston*". "The evening's clear-cut standout wasn't a Whitney song at all," he said. "It was her passionately soulful reading of Jennifer Holliday's 'I Am Changing'. Houston sang the song with such conviction and determination that you couldn't help wondering if she was

> *"When I decided to be a singer, my mother warned me I'd be alone a lot. Basically, we all are. Loneliness comes with life."*
>
> *Whitney Houston*

issuing a challenge to her audience to follow her in the new direction she is beginning to take."

Indeed, Whitney Houston was changing, becoming less a starlet or supermodel of the Eighties, and more a world-class entertainer. By the time of her next major tour, there would be no one to equal her success. US *Billboard* magazine named her their Artist of the Year in 1986, and in January 1987 she won an astonishing five American Music Awards. At the time, it seemed as if she had reached the peak of her career, and couldn't possibly improve on such success. But now we know otherwise.

Whitney's popularity with the public is equalled only by the respect she has earned within the music industry for her achievements.

Nothing But the Best

*n*o surprises here," said UK magazine *Smash Hits* in May 1987. "The great Whitney Houston announces her return from a long lay-off with her usual brilliant singing...Welcome back Ma'am!"

With the foot-tapping, Caribbean percussion and irresistible baritone backing vocals, 'I Wanna Dance With Somebody (Who Loves Me)' was the pop single of summer 1987. Everybody remembers the catchy, repetitive chorus and cute outro ("Dontcha wanna dance? Say ya wanna dance. Dontcha wanna dance?"). On the seemingly improvised bridge section Whitney gives a gorgeous giggle which spreads a brilliant ray of sunshine into the song. It is fun, classic pop, and was inevitably another Number 1 hit in the UK and US in May 1987, but that wasn't all.

'I Wanna Dance With Somebody (Who Loves Me)' was the Number 1 best-selling single of the year in the US, and in the UK it made Number 9 in the year-end chart—helped by

Whitney having performed the song on her one and only appearance on the legendary British TV show *Top of the Pops*. Written by Shannon Rubicam and George Merrill (of 'How Will I

Know' fame), the song had the dubious honour of being the fifth video clip ever transmitted by the satellite channel MTV Europe; but the greatest possible tribute to the classic hit was a Grammy Award for Best Female Pop Vocal Performance the following year.

Natural talent

In 1987, *Rolling Stone* summed up perfectly the master-plan behind the Arista Records team: "For her second album, Whitney Houston got the best that money can buy," read their review of her new LP, *Whitney*, "top producers (Narada Michael Walden, Jellybean, Kashif), proven commercial songwriters (Steinberg & Kelly, Michael Masser, Gerry Goffin) and a Richard Avedon cover photo. She was born with the rest." Contrary to the opinion of the cynics who accused her of being a "manufactured" star, this was a well-deserved recognition of Whitney's very real talent. Sure, she had the best people in the business working for

Whitney adopted hair extensions for a short-lived new look in 1987.

*Almost two dozen song-writers are credited for tracks on **Whitney**.*

Back in 1985, Whitney Houston told interviewers that she would be releasing a second album in the fall. In fact, the stunning success of her debut postponed the follow-up for nearly two years.

her. But no matter how talented were the boys in the back room, when Whitney Houston got behind the microphone, she was all alone.

Whitney

The opening track of *Whitney*, the effervescent 'I Wanna Dance With Somebody', seems to fulfill all the promise of the cover photograph, which shows the singer in a pose very different from that on her début album. Gone is the untouchable look, to be replaced by a far more approachable, down-to-earth Whitney Houston— it could almost be the cover for a Whitney Houston aerobics workout video.

The second track, 'Just The Lonely Talking Again', slows the pace down with a slushy love ballad by Sam Dees (who wrote Larry Graham's US megahit 'One In A Million You'). Three hit singles follow—'Love Will Save The Day', 'Didn't We Almost Have It All' and 'So Emotional'— followed by another ballad, 'Where You Are', a somewhat over-produced song of long-distance love. 'Love Is A Contact Sport' is probably the most popular of the tracks that never made it on to a 45, with a heavy kick drum driving the beat along and a very sexy vocal: "You gotta act untamed, If you wanna play the game, So grab my hand and ... SLAM!" It was an early sign that Whitney was keen to shake off her "Miss Clean" image and admit there might be more to love than romantic words.

One song that had been considered for Whitney's first album was returned to in 1987: Michael Masser and Gerry Goffin's 'You're Still

My Man'. It is a simple and unpretentious song, which Whitney brings to a rousing conclusion, but the lyrics are for once a little too clichéd to hold much meaning. On the other hand, the Isley Brothers' song 'For The Love Of You' (a 1976 UK Top 30 hit written at the peak of their success) is a superbly laid-back soul song, which forces Whitney to restrain her passion and relax into a gorgeous three-part harmony with herself on backing vocals. Although not released as a single, it was justifiably nominated for a Grammy for Best Female R&B Vocal Performance at the March 1988 awards.

Moving finale

'Where Do Broken Hearts Go' is followed by the closing track,

*Elaine Paige (**left**) inspired Whitney with her rendition of 'I Know Him So Well'.*

As her career progressed, Whitney relaxed into a more comfortable image to suit her buoyant character. "This tour is far more personalized for me," she said—right down to her designer costumes, custom-tailored by Fabrice.

Björn Ulvaeus. "I love the song," said Whitney. "I thought it was a classic, actually...I was in Germany and these two young ladies who originally sang the song [Elaine Paige and Barbara Dickson] were in the dressing-room next to me and I could hear them singing it...And then, two years later, we were playing through some material for the new album and someone asked me 'Do you like this song?' And there it was!"

On Whitney's version, she is joined on lead vocals by her mother, which brings the album to a very moving climax. On the sleeve notes Whitney thanks her "Mommy" warmly for her contribution: "What a joy and an honour to have had the opportunity to be able to do something with you that will be a treasure for me."

'I Know Him So Well', taken from the West End/Broadway hit musical *Chess* by lyricist Tim Rice and Abba stars Benny Andersson and

*"Half of the songs
on the first album I
didn't consider great
songs. But singers
can make them
great, of course."*

Eight-figure sales

Smash Hits proved to be somewhat ignorant of Whitney's popularity on the British pop scene when reviewer Ian Cranna described *Whitney* as "groansomely boring", giving it a pitiful four marks out of ten. Yet despite this scathing review, the album's sales were undamaged.

Whitney was a massive success, hitting the UK Number 1 and going to the top of the US album charts in the first week of release, making her the first female solo artist ever to do so. The album sold five million copies in its first six months of release. It held a fleeting joint record for the most US Number 1 singles from one album (four), which was beaten by Michael Jackson a year later. It became the Number 2 best-selling US album of 1987, and Number 3 in the UK's top sellers of the year. According to Russell Ash's book *The Top 10 of Music*, *Whitney* is also the Number 10 best-selling album of all time in the Netherlands! Meanwhile, *Whitney Houston* was selling almost as rapidly, making Number 8 in the year's US albums and topping 13 million sales by the end of 1987.

Montreux star

In May, Whitney Houston, along with more than 60 other singers and bands from around the world, appeared at the Montreux Pop Festival in Switzerland. Characteristically staying out of

> *"I didn't just run into this and say, 'I want to be a star and a singer.' My mother wasn't going to go for that...So I had to finish school."*
>
> *Whitney Houston*

the limelight at her hotel in Lausanne, Whitney surfaced only twice during the week, for a press conference and a single performance. Seen by *Smash Hits* to be wearing an "extremely glittery silver and gold bracelet" with the word "Whitney" spelled out in diamonds, she was asked if it was a gift, and she admitted bashfully that she had bought it herself—although she did not let on how much she had paid for it.

Asked at the press conference if fame was turning her head, she said: "I'm coping with it. The only way that it affects me is that I don't have as much time as I used to by myself." She reiterated that fame was no big surprise to her: "What you have to remember," she said simply, "is that I took my time with this. I didn't just run into this and say 'I want to be a star and a singer.' My

mother wasn't going to go for that...So I had to finish school; that's all that matters when you're young. So I think I've had my fun in my teen years. There's not anything I particularly miss."

Major US tour

Whitney's 1987 summer tour of the States was her most extensive to date, comprising multiple shows in 25 cities. She opened the tour in Tampa, Florida on July 4 and wound up in Montreal, Canada, on August 28. It was a gruelling schedule—"By the end of a tour you really understand the phrase 'There's no place like home'!" she said.

The setting remained "in the round", but this time the song list was far more rich with two full

> *"She can deliver
> a gospel rasp,
> a velvety coo, a floating
> soprano and a
> cheerleader's whoop"*
>
> Jon Pareles,
> New York Times

albums to draw on. Cissy Houston often joined Whitney to sing back-up vocals on the gospel standard 'I Believe', and then remained on stage for the big-build-up ballads 'Didn't We Almost Have It All' and 'The Greatest Love Of All'. Jon Pareles in the *New York Times* lavishly praised Whitney's sold-out shows at Madison Square Garden, calling her "an encyclopedic, restless virtuoso" whose voice incorporated "everyone from Aretha Franklin to Barbra Streisand to Diana Ross to Al Green". He continued: "She can deliver a gospel rasp, a velvety coo, a floating soprano and a cheerleader's whoop," in an article titled: "Whitney Houston Can Sing Up a Storm".

When Whitney turned 24, she was already a superstar and on a major tour of the USA.

Whitney told **Rolling Stone** magazine: "My mother was always encouraging me to sing. She told me to use my God-given talent. She said. 'If you don't use it. God will give it to someone else.'"

'Didn't We Almost Have It All'

Described by Caroline Sullivan in the UK *Guardian* newspaper as "irredeemably gooey", Whitney Houston's fifth US Number 1 single is a brilliant ballad—another from the pen of Michael Masser—which Whitney performs with great passion. By the final line of the third verse Whitney's voice is so loud that it is shaking the speakers as she sings: "Once you know what love is, you never let it end." It is a touching recollection of a love affair that has gone too far, and was nominated for a Grammy Award for the 1987 Song of the Year.

However, the song itself was among those noted by critics who claimed that Whitney's performance lacked the pain of the heartbreak she sang about, and that she could never truly be called a soul singer, because she did not sing from her soul. *Smash Hits* again demonstrated their lack of judgement by writing: "She's lumbered with an incredibly bland, soulless voice. There's never any emotion in the way she sings." To this accusation, Whitney was quick to retort: "I do sing from my soul," she said. "I'm only 24, so I haven't gone through as much as Billie Holiday. I wasn't a drug addict, I've never felt dark and melancholic. I had a good childhood, no tragedies, and I can only sing from my own life experiences."

A bizarre honour from the Caribbean island of Grenada—Whitney Houston postage stamps.

'So Emotional'

'So Emotional' was written by the hit-making team William Steinberg and Tom Kelly, the duo behind Madonna's erotic smash 'Like A Virgin', 'True Colors' for Cyndi Lauper and 'Alone' for Heart. It is a crossover rock/pop/dance-floor single, with a pounding rock back-beat and a raunchy lead break played by Cornado Rustici on guitar synth; it takes Whitney's voice from the highest pitch to the lowest funky growl. It swung into the top spot in the States one more time and made it to Number 5 in the UK. It was her sixth US Number 1 single in a row, equalling a record previously shared only by the Beatles and the Bee Gees. The single was Whitney's first step away from the "tame" sound of love ballads into something more raw and gritty, and although she has never left the romantic songs behind, she has gone on to spread her wings wider and wider. Even heavy metal singer Zodiac Mindwarp (guest singles reviewer in *Smash Hits*) was impressed by the record. "This is a good record," he wrote, "and very *tough* for Whitney. She's got wonderful legs and she's a great singer."

"Sometimes I only want to be a regular person...I say to myself, 'I'm not Whitney today,' and I don't think about her world. I just walk around as if I'm a normal person."—Whitney Houston

Whitney's fabulous ballad 'Where Do Broken Hearts Go' was her seventh consecutive US Number 1.

A Very Special Christmas

A Very Special Christmas (1987) is an album of exclusive "Christmassy" recordings by celebrated artists compiled to raise money for Special Olympics International. The beautiful red-and-gold sleeve was designed by US artist Keith Haring, and the album features tracks by Madonna, Bon Jovi, Sting, U2, the Pointer Sisters, Eurythmics, Bruce Springsteen and others.

Whitney contributed the gospel song 'Do You Hear What I Hear?' aided by vocals from Darlene Love, a veteran of Phil Spector's Sixties pop factory. The song reappeared on CD versions of 'I Will Always Love You' in 1992.

A new record!

Although it is a powerfully emotional ballad, 'Where Do Broken Hearts Go' is likely to be remembered not for its music and lyrics but for breaking a long-standing US chart record. Seizing the top spot once more in February 1988, Whitney was the first artist in history to have seven consecutive *Billboard* Number 1 singles.

In March 1988 Whitney was awarded the Grammy for Best Female Pop Vocal Performance for 'I Wanna Dance With Somebody'. At the awards she cried out "I love you Clive! I love you Arista!" and later she said to reporters "I can't tell you how I feel. It's so...emotional!"

> "*I always had the feeling my singing career would work out. Oh, yeah, I just knew it.*"
>
> *Whitney Houston*

'I Wanna Dance With Somebody' won Whitney her second Grammy Award, for Best Female Pop Vocal Performance. It also won Narada Michael Walden an Award for Best Producer.

New Directions

By May 1988 Whitney Houston had earned $45 million (£30 million) from record sales, but it was in this month that her incredible record-breaking streak of US Number 1 hits was to come to an end with 'Love Will Save The Day', the final single cut from *Whitney*. It was the only track from the album to be produced by Madonna's collaborator and one-time lover Jellybean Benitez, who told *Smash Hits* in December 1987: "Of all the famous people I've ever worked with, Whitney Houston is my favourite. She's a lot of fun." The single reached Number 9 in the US and Number 10 in the UK—an impressive success, by most standards...but Whitney Houston's standards are higher than most.

"In anyone's eyes she is a star—spangled, glitzed-out and embarrassingly ecstatic—yet still a star." Lucy O'Brien. NME, October 1986.

> *"Of all the famous people I've ever worked with, Whitney Houston is my favourite. She's a lot of fun."*
>
> *Jellybean Benitez*

On the road again

Meanwhile, Whitney had reached the UK on her latest world tour, making appearances at Birmingham's NEC (five consecutive nights) and London's Wembley Arena. The Wembley dates accounted for yet another broken record—a run of nine shows, which was the most by any solo performer at that time.

The tour was once again "in the round", and Whitney was led through the crowd to the stage to begin the set with a rousing 'Didn't We Almost Have It All', usually dressed in a long, plain coat, which she then removed to reveal a black silk halter top and knee-length pink satin skirt. In the *Guardian* Adam Sweeting marvelled at her pristine beauty: "Despite the occasional

Whitney made an effort to communicate with the crowd, although this often invited heckling, which seemed to make her feel uneasy —she still had a lot to learn about the price of fame.

gleam of perspiration," he said, "she looked throughout as though she'd just stepped out of a hat box."

Reportedly inspired by a visit to Michael Jackson's extravagant Bad Tour in New York, the show had a stronger accent on movement and variety than ever before, and a team of dancers took the stage for the faster numbers. A passionate version of '(You Make Me Feel Like A) Natural Woman' saw Whitney alone on stage, but for other numbers she was joined by her saxophonist, or a keyboard player with a portable synthesizer.

Nelson Mandela's birthday party

Organized by Artists Against Apartheid, a British awareness-raising pressure group, the Nelson Mandela Tribute Concert in London in June 1988 was intended to be something of a "Live Aid 2". The world's pop stars came together for one spectacular 11-hour gig to remind the public of the long imprisonment of Nelson Mandela in South Africa. Whitney Houston, normally wary of involvement with political issues, was crucially important to the credibility of the venture, as a representative of America's major black talent. Barry Marshall, promoter of

Whitney conducts the audience of more than 70,000 at Wembley Stadium.

Singing to free Nelson Mandela on June 11, 1988.

Whitney's massive European tour, offered to talk to the star, and persuaded her to postpone a gig already planned for Milan, Italy on June 11.

Whitney was joined by Phil Collins, Al Green, George Michael, Peter Gabriel, Roberta Flack, Stevie Wonder, and dozens of other celebrities, and the show was transmitted live on British television and radio by the BBC. On US television the Fox Network aired a controversially "edited" version which strategically removed many of the references to the concert's political motive, using the evasive title "Freedomfest".

It soon became clear that apartheid was an issue that Whitney Houston felt very strongly about. Apparently, during her brief time as a model, Whitney had refused to promote any company that had branches in South Africa, and it was even suggested that Whitney had been in communication with Nelson Mandela's wife, Winnie.

You lucky guys!
Before the show even began, Whitney was the subject of an unusual tribute from South Africa. On the afternoon of the concert, the Anti-Apartheid Movement distributed a statement from Ahmed Kathrada, who at 58 was the youngest of the ANC rebels who were sentenced

to life imprisonment along with Mandela: "You lucky guys. What I wouldn't give just to listen to Whitney Houston!" said Ahmed. "I must have told you that she has long been mine and Walter's [Walter Sisulu—fellow prisoner aged 76] top favourite. In our love and admiration for Whitney we are prepared to be second to none!"

Perhaps Whitney was aware of her glowing review, because she entertained with brimming energy. It was a disappointment for some—an earlier announcement had promised an "all gospel" set, which never materialized—but the audience were treated to a duet by Whitney and her mother, the gospel song 'I Believe', which Whitney dedicated to "Nelson Mandela and his family, and for all of my South African brothers and sisters".

Collaboration

As the new decade approached, Whitney's career was quieter than usual, though she was far from idle. In 1988 she had contributed vocals to a song called 'Hold Up The Light' from BeBe (Benjamin) & CeCe (Priscilla) Winans' album *Heaven*. Also, while performing live in London, she recorded

Nelson Mandela was finally released in 1990 and appeared on the very same stage to address another capacity crowd.

"The main joy with Whitney is there's such a chemistry," said BeBe Winan. "It's almost as if she was born and raised with us, because the energy she gives is the same."

"Don't judge a book by its cover. There's a part of me that's very relaxed, very jeans and T-shirt, very kooky."

Whitney Houston

the title track to an Arista Records compilation album in commemoration of the 1988 Olympics in Los Angeles. The album was called *One Moment In Time*, and the eponymous single was yet another Number 1 hit for Whitney on both sides of the Atlantic. Written by Albert Hammond, the man behind Starship's mega-hit 'Nothing's Gonna Stop Us Now' and Leo Sayer's classic Seventies weepie 'When I Need You', the single was one of the Top 20 hits of the year in the UK and Whitney was nominated for a Grammy for Best Female Pop Vocal Performance. Sadly the record was deleted in 1990.

In 1989 Whitney's voice was heard on a new single by a lady she once knew as "Aunt Ree"—

Right: *With Blair Underwood, star of LA Law, on stage at the Avery Fisher Hall, New York.*

one of her mother's oldest friends, Aretha Franklin. Her album *Through The Storm* featured a funky soul groove called 'It Isn't, It Wasn't, It Ain't Never Gonna Be' (a kind of sequel to Aretha's collaboration with The Eurythmics on 'Sisters Are Doing It For Themselves'), which was released as a single in September 1989, reaching Number 41 in the US and 29 in Britain.

Meanwhile, Whitney was considering an even more diverse move—a career in the movies. The scripts were flooding in, with potential co-stars rumoured to include Robert De Niro and Eddie Murphy (with whom Whitney was said to be romantically "connected" for a while). But the right film had not come along.

Going back to basics

In the summer of 1989, she joined her friends the Winans on a tour of the US as a back-up singer. The tour was perfectly timed for Whitney. Not only was it an opportunity to return to her gospel roots,

Right: Eddie Murphy and Whitney Houston out on the town, feeding the rumours that they were having a relationship.

but it was also a chance to sing without feeling the pressure of the audience's expectations. The Winans' following was a predominantly gospel crowd, so Whitney was able to relax in the background and just let go. Whitney's cousin Dionne Warwick and soul singer Luther Vandross also guested at some of the Winans' shows.

Taste of something new

Whitney's next single, in October 1990, was the title track of her forthcoming third LP, released later the same year. 'I'm Your Baby Tonight' was a clear indication that this was going to be a relentless dance album. Whitney gives the song a potent sound with throaty, soulful growls and uninhibited squeals and screams. It makes a perfect single and a perfect opening track, as Whitney wraps up the instant thrill of love at first sight with the irresistible, sexy beat of a pop song. No wonder the song was so popular—only a woman with this much class could make a song about a passionate one-night stand sound like a love song!

'I'm Your Baby Tonight' was nominated for a Grammy for Best Female Pop Vocal Performance in 1991, but was beaten by newcomer Mariah

Whitney was becoming accustomed to receiving Grammy Awards when she was nominated again in 1991—though this time she didn't collect.

> *"They don't say I sound like Mariah Carey, they say Mariah Carey sounds like me, you dig what I'm saying?"*
>
> *Whitney Houston*

In **I'm Your Baby Tonight** *Whitney seized upon the many fresh sounds of the late Eighties, from the cool toughness of hip-hop to the hot raunchiness of the funk revival. She proved she would not be left behind by the new decade.*

Carey with 'Vision Of Love'—one of many new artists who had surfaced in the late Eighties as pretenders to Whitney's throne. However, the competition was not something that troubled Whitney, confident in her own charisma. As she explained later: "People who go out and buy me, buy me for me. Furthermore, I came out first anyways [laughs]…anybody that's gonna come has definitely got to come after. They don't say I sound like Mariah Carey, they say Mariah Carey sounds like me, you dig what I'm saying?"

Long-awaited release

To call *I'm Your Baby Tonight* long-awaited would be one of pop music's greatest understatements. Despite Whitney's regular appearances in the singles chart, the world had been waiting three and a half years for a new Whitney Houston album. Released in 1990, *I'm Your Baby Tonight* represented a major turning-point in Whitney's career as she launched herself into the Nineties with a renewed passion for pop music in all its different forms.

I'm Your Baby Tonight

I'm Your Baby Tonight kicks off with three very different singles: the irresistibly danceable title track, the hip-hop influenced 'My Name Is Not Susan', and the powerful 'All The Man That I Need', in which the extraordinary scream of the saxophone follows Whitney's lead as the song builds into a wave of adoration. It became Whitney's ninth US Number 1 hit single in December 1990.

Above: "When LA and Babyface worked with me they were really surprised. It was like 'Hey, you're really funky, you're bad!' " —Whitney Houston

Left: Whitney at Arista Records' 15th anniversary celebration, with Clive Davis and a host of celebrities.

'Lover for Life' is a light-hearted, bouncy pop song on the surface, but its lyrics have great charm, as they describe a love affair as if it were a court case: "You've heard my testimony, you've seen my evidence, hey it's a crime of passion, in every sense...will you sentence me to be your lover for life?"

Bobby Brown's producers LA Reid and Babyface worked on two of the tracks, 'Anymore' and 'Miracle'. Their influence is particularly apparent on 'Anymore', a soulful, laid-back groove, in which Whitney's strong side creeps back to reject yet another suitor who does not fit the bill, and her Jacksonesque vocals prove that, contrary to her romantic image, she can be as bad as any man! 'Miracle' sees Whitney as the glamorous, heart-rending balladeer once more. The longest song on the album, it pushes the scope of Whitney's voice to its fullest extent.

'I Belong to You' borrows the catchy hook from 'Just Be Good To Me' by the SOS Band. One of three tracks produced by Narada Michael Walden, the song has his trademark slick arrangements with

Whitney presented Stevie Wonder with the Carousel of Hope Award at the Children's Diabetes Foundation in 1990.

soothing sax and melodic rhythm guitar—
it was released as a single in 1992, with little chart success. 'Who Do You Love' was
Whitney's first collaboration with soul
crooner Luther Vandross, and the sleeve
notes promise that we can look forward to
more. Whitney's mother is reportedly his
favourite singer, and he invited her to sing
on his first two albums.

Singing with Stevie

'We Didn't Know' is another first-time collaboration, this time with Motown songwriting genius Stevie Wonder. Putting two
megastars in the studio together can be a
dangerous experiment, but the result of this
combination sounds totally natural. If anything, 'We Didn't Know' is dominated by
Stevie's own soul signature, but he and
Whitney sound superb together. How this
song failed to be released as a single remains
a mystery. Surely it would have been massive?

'After We Make Love' is probably more
memorable for its risqué post-coital title than

*"There's a direct line between singing ballads and
singing about the love God has for us and we have
for Him. Love is love is love, you know."—Whitney
Houston*

its rather schmaltzy lyrics (an uncomfortable marriage of religion and sex) but the closing number 'I'm Knockin'', is right back on course. It marks Whitney's first attempt at co-production, with her musical director Rickey Minor, and the song a perfect choice for her to work on. With a melody almost exclusively provided by Whitney's own vocals—both lead and back-up—'I'm Knockin'' gave her the chance to play around with her own voice in the studio, a useful experience for the future.

The album was relatively unsuccessful in the UK and US, reaching Number 4 and Number 3 respectively. Ian McCann in UK music paper *NME* gave the album an almost unprecedented zero out of ten, commenting with an air of disappointment: "Whitney sings better than ever, but so what?... Tomorrow night, Whitney, be your own baby and shock us all." It is likely that the sharp change of pace was a disappointment to many of the fans who had made the first two albums so very successful. However, if *I'm Your Baby Tonight* was not the album that the world wanted her to make, it was certainly a big step towards it, and those same fans were soon to come flooding back to her—and more besides.

Whitney uses her concert appearances to reinterpret her hit singles and show off her startling vocal dexterity.

Charity work

In 1991, Whitney made good use of her celebrity by raising a great deal of money for charity. She was invited to begin the ceremonies of the 25th Superbowl at Joe Robbie Stadium, Miami, Florida by singing the traditional anthem 'The Star-Spangled Banner'. Although her performance was pre-recorded, it was a definitive version of the uplifting hymn, and public demand inevitably led to the release of a single and video.

In true Whitney Houston style, the record went to the US Number 20 spot and raised $500,000 (£335,000) for civilian victims of the Gulf War. In May Whitney performed live via satellite at The Simple Truth gig at London's Wembley Arena to raise money for Kurdish refugees, and was noted by the American Red Cross in recognition of her fund-raising efforts.

On stage with brother Gary Garland.

With US politician and civil rights veteran Jesse Jackson.

Whitney Houston Live

Those fans who had so far been denied the chance to see Whitney perform live were finally able to get the next best thing in April 1991. *Whitney Houston Live* was a colourful concert recorded at the naval air station in Norfolk, Virginia, on the east coast of the USA, on March 31 that year. The concert was first transmitted by the Home Box Office (HBO) on US television, under the title *Welcome Home Heroes with Whitney Houston*, and it caused a small controversy at the time.

To absent friends

The Norfolk show was in many ways a preview of Whitney's 1991 tour set list. To the audience of servicemen and women, the Gulf War had been both a chance to serve their country and a terrifying experience in which the lives of friends, family and lovers were at stake. "It's so good to see you all home safe and sound," said Whitney. "From what I understand, there are still a few of our troops left over there—so this one's for them, too!" After a roar of applause, Whitney continued: "That's right—until they all come home. Until they *all* come

On January 12, 1991, Whitney received an award for distinguished achievement from the American Cinema Award Foundation in Los Angeles. At the awards ceremony she shared the stage with movie legend Gregory Peck.

home. I think this next song's gonna describe... how you felt when you took your loved one in your arms—and I know you made love all night long. Ooh, I know you did!"—and Kirk Whalum's saxophone began to pick out the bluesy melody of her next song, 'Saving All My Love'.

Pop tunes and songs of love

Whitney's dancers joined her for the cheerful 'How Will I Know', and with the backing singers picking up the melody, there was plenty of room for Whitney's own bluesy variations on the song. Skipping off-stage, Whitney prepared herself for the second part of the show with a lightning change into a beautiful red evening gown. Sweeping back in along the raised metal walkway and daintily down the steps, she accepted cards from the more presumptuous men in the audience, coyly asking them, "I'm gonna sing you some love songs. Is that all right?" Almost unaccompanied at first, but for the gentle voice of a piano in the background, Whitney launched into a slow and emotional version of 'Didn't We Almost Have It All', which built into a crescendo, imperceptibly changing into a medley with the Burt Bacharach— Hal David standard 'A House Is Not A Home' and 'Where Do Broken Hearts Go'.

The show-stopper was 'All The Man That I Need'. Clasping a towel in one hand as she sang, her face and plunging neckline glistened with perspiration as she closed her eyes tightly with the intensity of the moment.

"Behind the marketing is a gospel-stung larynx that can almost bring you to your knees"—Damon Wise,
Sounds*, May 1988*

Party atmosphere

The show's third act began with the pounding drum beat of 'My Name Is Not Susan' as Whitney and her dancers worked out on the raised gangway at the rear of the stage. In peppermint green leggings, boots and matching mini-dress with glittery silver "W.H." motif, Whitney used a radio microphone and headset to make this final part of the show very mobile. For 'My Name Is Not Susan' the dancers wore brightly coloured linen suits, and Whitney, as always, proved that her voice was strong enough to last the distance, no matter what the pace.

Taking a break from the dance numbers, Whitney was alone under the spotlight for a few moments as she sang an operatic, jazzy love song called 'A Song For You'. However, the stage was soon alive with colour and light for the brilliant gospel hymn 'Revelation' as Whitney called out, "Put your hands together for the Lord," and the audience willingly complied. A heart-warming tune, 'Revelation', gave Whitney the chance to introduce her band and bring a series of brief solos from each performer into the show.

Whitney's 1991 tour earned a mixed reception from the critics.

The big finish

After another change of costume into a spectacular, off-the-shoulder blue satin dress, Whitney grabbed from somewhere an ungainly sailor's cap as the opening melody of 'Who Do You Love' began, and wore it throughout the track. Joined on stage by the four dancers, Whitney turned the song into another stomping workout. With 'I'm Your Baby Tonight' getting the same treatment, the set was completed with a version of 'Greatest Love Of All'. Whitney basked in her perfect moment as a little boy was shyly coaxed on to the stage to share the limelight. It was a stirring and mesmerizing performance, made especially potent by the atmosphere of wartime thanksgiving in the crowd.

Cynics in the audience

Following the transmission of the concert on US TV, renowned critic Robert Hilburn criticized Whitney Houston in the *LA Times* for using the Gulf War as an opportunity to exploit the emotions of the families and servicemen involved, commenting that Ms Houston's motivation for the performance was suspiciously unclear. However, to its credit, the newspaper allowed HBO producer Anthony Eaton to redress the balance two weeks later. "We built a show for the returning servicemen and women," wrote Eaton, "and they

came. They came and they pretty much blew the top off Hangar LP-2 in Norfolk." In an attempt to "justify" the homecoming performance, Eaton pointed to the ecstatic reaction of the crowd. "We had sailors dancing with army lieutenants," he claimed with pride, "air-force fliers singing along with the coastguard, boy soldiers bashfully handing flowers to Whitney on stage, proud families with their reunited moms and dads and, of course, marines hanging off the rafters. That night it felt like Babe Ruth pointing to left field, Lindbergh landing in Paris, Martin Luther King's speech at the Washington Monument." Finishing with an indignant rebuff, Eaton praised Whitney's integrity and sincerity. "Contrary to Hilburn's comments, Whitney is a mysterious figure. In an age of fiercely ambitious artists trying whatever tricks they can to catch and hold the public's attention, it can be confusing to see an artist whose stage production is built around her outstanding vocal performance."

Mixed reactions

Whitney's 1991 world tour was far from a disaster, but the reaction of the paying customers was mixed—not surprising after the relatively poor sales of her third album. In the *New York Times*,

At the American Cinema Awards. January 1991.

Peter Watrous was scathing in his review of her return bout at Madison Square Garden in July. Noting that the venue was far from full, he claimed that the concert-goers were "mostly underwhelmed" and suggested that Whitney displayed a distinct lack of commitment to the performance. She "isn't a natural performer", he said, "and she hasn't in any way mastered the large-scale rhetoric of passion needed to convince

"In an age of fiercely ambitious artists trying whatever tricks they can to catch and hold the public's attention, it can be confusing to see an artist whose stage production is built around her outstanding vocal performance."

HBO producer Anthony Eaton

a huge hall of her sincerity. In a form that demands acrobatics, she's ungainly at best, looking distinctly ill-at-ease, as if she had suddenly awakened to find herself in someone else's body." The same critic sourly described her band as "clattering around like a drunk in a kitchen," and felt that they "managed to drown out any singing she might have wanted to do, which apparently wasn't much anyway". Watrous did concede that those songs that featured Whitney's

The American Music Awards are voted for by the general public, so Whitney has almost won more than she can carry!

characteristic "deep blues gospel tonalities" were distinctly different, proving "that in the right circumstances she can be as athletic a singer as anybody in pop music."

Back in the UK
When the show moved to the UK a month later—with huge light show, back-projections, video screens, moving catwalks, firework displays and all—some of the critics were less than charitable. In the *Guardian*, Caroline Sullivan pointedly referred to Whitney's dalliance with political controversy: "Originally planned for Spring, Whitney Houston's tour was postponed when the little contretemps in the Gulf gave her a sore throat." The gigs at Birmingham's NEC and Wembley Arena in London were almost sold out, but Sullivan compared the show to a cabaret: "In her sparkly catwoman suit she could have been Shirley Bassey giving it some at the Palladium."

However, the same critic also confessed to witnessing one of the most stirring soul music performances she had seen on stage as Whitney Houston sang the emotional 'Didn't We Almost Have It All'. "Unexpectedly, her hauteur cracked," wrote Ms Sullivan. "She broke into a sweat—surely a physiological impossibility?—as she caressed the lyric. At the end she hung her head and, if a video screen did not lie, cried. It was an extraordinarily moving moment, the more so for its incongruity. 'All The Man That I Need' eased to a gospelly crescendo that was similarly startling. At its climax the singer seemed to be in a reverie. This was Whitney! It was exhilarating to hear a world-class voice deployed, for once, on material worthy of it."

All the Man that I Need

Robert Baresford Brown was just 14 years old when New Edition hit the UK Number 1 spot with 'Candy Girl'. The five-piece group from Boston, Massachusetts was an Eighties answer to the Jackson 5: light-weight, radio-friendly pop singers with universal appeal. Splitting from their manager—pop entrepreneur Maurice Starr—in 1984, they signed a major recording deal with MCA Records. New Edition released four albums featuring Bobby Brown: *Candy Girl* (1983), *New Edition* (1984), *All For Love* (1985) and *Under The Blue Moon* (1986). The records spawned several hit singles, including the US Number 4 'Cool It Now' and a revival of the Doo-Wop standard 'Earth Angel', which reached Number 3 in the States.

Although remaining with MCA, Bobby Brown went solo in 1986. His first solo album *King Of*

Six years his elder, but Whitney is every bit the equal of Bobby Brown's raunchy image.

Stage (1986) made little impact, although the single 'Girlfriend' was a massive R&B chart hit. However, his next album, *Don't Be Cruel* (1989), produced by LA Reid & Babyface, topped the US chart, and on the strength of the US Number 1 single 'My Prerogative' it remained in the album chart for 97 weeks.

On the crest of a wave of success, Bobby Brown toured the States extensively in 1989, wowing audiences with his relentless dance routines. The US Number 3 hit single 'Every Little Step' was followed closely by 'On Our Own', tied in with one of the summer's major films *Ghostbusters 2*, which made a UK and US Top 5 hit. 'Every Little Step' was the winner of the year's Grammy Award for Best R&B Vocal Performance. Another sell-out world tour followed in 1990, which included eight nights at Wembley Arena in London. His most recent album, *Bobby,* features deeper, more introspective lyrics and a broad range of Nineties dance sounds.

New Edition's record sales in the UK were unable to match their success in America, and their last Gallup chart entry was with 'Mr Telephone Man' in 1985.

Beauty and the beast

Bobby Brown has a bad reputation. Having fathered three illegitimate children before first meeting Whitney at the Soul Train awards in 1989,

Bobby's dancing got him into trouble at a show in Georgia in 1989, where he was arrested for "giving a sexually explicit performance harmful to minors".

it seems fair to say that Bobby had lived life to the full. So, has Whitney really tamed the wild man of rap? If she can be believed, the answer is no—he was never the wild man to begin with. "I just want people to understand something," she said in 1993. "My husband has never, never disrespected any woman...He's a respectable human being. He was raised with respect. And I

"So why does the world just keep on doggin' me/I have to leave it all behind/Coz there's gotta be a way/For me to escape all this nonsense"—a blunt reaction to the tabloid press in 'Get Away'.

just wish they would stop trying to make him out to be this man who just goes around and arbitrarily says, 'I want her, and I'm gonna screw her.' "

However, "they"—meaning newspapers and magazines, of course—are never likely to stop their speculation, as she knows. Sensational weekly American tabloid magazine the *National Enquirer* ran a story as recently as December 1993 with the headline "Whitney Houston Blasts Cheating Hubby". In it, "insiders" claimed that Whitney had accused Bobby of adultery with at least one of his old girlfriends and a "beautiful black TV actress". The same magazine has on more than one occasion accused Whitney of having a gay relationship with her close friend Robyn Crawford, whom she met at summer camp at the age of 17.

Wedding bells
On July 18, 1992, Whitney Houston was married to Bobby Brown at her

The veil of superstardom drops briefly as the newlyweds are snapped in a moment of intimacy.

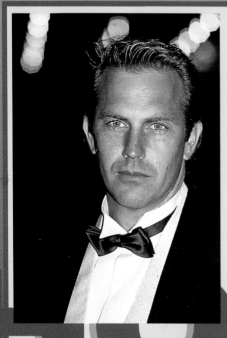

"You cross me up this time, Rachel, and I swear I'll kill you myself."—Kevin Costner as Frank Farmer in **The Bodyguard**

$2.8 million (£1.87 million) five-acre estate in New Jersey. The bride and groom both wore white. Whitney's hand-embroidered lace gown cost $40,000 (£27,000), and her twelve-strong wedding party were all dressed in purple (apparently her favourite colour). The ceremony was followed by a reception for 800, after which the happy couple jetted off for Nice, via London, travelling by Concorde. Whitney was already pregnant with their first child.

So far they have collaborated musically only once, in a duet, 'Something In Common', released as a single in January 1994. *Rolling Stone* said simply: "This duet shouldn't work. The fact that they're mismatched—vocally that is—forces them to feel each other out, testing their stylistic limits." Not only does the song challenge their very different talents, it is also a landmark in their romance, as Bobby sings "Girl you know it's you that I adore," to which Whitney replies, sweetly: "And there's no one in this world that I love more."

Changing track

Back in September 1987, *Rolling Stone* magazine reported Whitney's interest in a complementary career: "Now that topping the charts has become old hat, Whitney wants to establish herself as an actor. 'It's inevitable,' she says. 'I'm sure that music will turn into acting. It could happen at any

point.'" Apparently, Whitney had been offered a part in a movie version of the hit Broadway musical *Dreamgirls*, but this was not destined to be her silver-screen début.

Clean-cut hero

Kevin Costner emerged from the Eighties as Hollywood's most important and versatile superstar. Narrowly missing his first chance at fame, Kevin's part was cut from Lawrence Kasdan's seminal coming-of-age movie *The Big Chill* in 1983. However, his first leading role came with *Fandango* in 1985, closely followed by Kasdan's enthusiastic western *Silverado*. In 1987 Costner struck gold as the strong and sensitive Pentagon officer thrust into an international minefield of crime and espionage in *No Way Out*. As the striking, clean-cut naval man he was sexy and brooding, but most of all, in the

Whitney has expressed an interest in acting in a cop movie. "I like the idea of having a gun and hiding behind walls."

Costner's on-screen power seems to come from a brooding inner drive—on the surface his characters may be distant, insensitive, officious or angry, but deep inside, they always have a strong, intuitive sense of right and wrong.

film-maker Brian De Palma, portrayed him as a fictional Elliot Ness fighting evil in prohibition-era Chicago. However, as Costner moved into the Nineties he truly discovered his role in the Hollywood star system.

A stunning début

His first job as a director was on the epic western Dances with Wolves, a breathtaking film in which Costner plays a soldier alone on the frontier, learning the ways of the Sioux Indians. The spectacular three-hour film was widely praised by critics and showed Costner's fans a very different side of his talent. Working on a limited budget (he gave up part of his fee to reduce production costs), Costner made Dances with Wolves into an unforgettable cinematic experience, and at the US Academy Awards in 1991 he took away the Oscars for Best Picture and Best Director.

Only days after the completion of *Dances with Wolves*, Kevin started shooting *Robin Hood: Prince of Thieves*, a $50 million (£35 million) film

thrill of the chase, he was a man of quick-witted action. More leading roles soon followed in the baseball movies *Bull Durham* and *Field of Dreams* in 1987 and 1988 respectively. A year later, *The Untouchables*, directed by all-action

Grand and extravagant, but ultimately very vulnerable. Rachel Marron in **The Bodyguard**.

directed by his old friend and *Fandango* director Kevin Reynolds, which went on to be a runaway box-office success. Costner's next role was in the controversial political thriller *JFK*, directed by Oliver Stone (*Platoon, Born on the Fourth of*

"Frank Farmer is heroic because he has a code and sticks to it," says Costner. *"There is...a consistency to Rachel, because she is just as tough in her world... But Frank shows her that she can relax and feel safe with him, and that changes their relationship."*

July), in which he reconstructed District Attorney Jim Garrison's investigation into the assassination of President Kennedy. Like so many of Costner's most successful characterizations, Garrison was seen to have a higher purpose than

> *"I was amazed at the incredible aura he generated. Like all great actors, his charisma almost swamped me, and I was gulping and stuttering like a kid."*
>
> *Whitney on Kevin Costner*

mundane detective work. He had a quest, an all-encompassing purpose in life. For Elliot Ness in *The Untouchables,* the motivation was the defence of law and order. Likewise in *The Bodyguard*, in which Costner played poker-faced Frank Farmer, the hero's reason for living is complete dedication to

Whitney with Kevin Costner and his wife, Cindy.

work—he was the paragon of professionalism, ready to die to save the life of his employer.

Costner's on-screen power seems to come from a brooding inner drive—on the surface he may be distant, insensitive, officious or angry, but deep inside his characters always have a strongly intuitive sense of right and wrong. So, although the good guy does not always win, at least the audience is left knowing who the hero really is.

Despite achieving cumulative box-office takings throughout his career of $1.3 billion (£870 million), much of the boyish, down-to-earth personality shines through the glitter. Costner's 15-year marriage to his wife Cindy has lasted longer than most Hollywood careers. He has three children, Annie, Lily and Joe. He drives a Shelby Mustang car with the numberplate "Crash D"—the very car that his character drove in *Bull Durham*. He has his own film-making company, Tig Productions, which was responsible for both *Dances with Wolves* and *The*

The start of the love affair: Rachel is rescued from the stage when the crowd goes out of control.

Bodyguard. Somehow, amid the extraordinary world of Hollywood, Kevin Costner remains just an ordinary guy.

I wanna act with somebody
When Kevin Costner's offer came along, it seemed too good to be true. Whitney told *Rolling Stone*: "I got a call saying that there was a script that Kevin Costner had, called *The Bodyguard*, that he wanted me to do. I went, 'Yeah, sure.' " Was she really ready to perform alongside the biggest Hollywood star of the moment? "I wanted to do some acting, you know," Whitney told US movie magazine *Premiere* in 1992, "but I didn't think it would be this major."

It took a considerable time for Kevin to persuade Whitney to be his leading lady. "I was scared," she told *Rolling Stone* in 1993. "It took me two years to decide to do it. I kind of waited too long for Kevin. I think it got on his nerves. He called one day and said, 'Listen, are you going to do this movie with me or not?' I told him about my fears; I said: 'I'm afraid. I don't want to go out there and fall.' He said 'I promise you I will not let you fall. I will help you.' And he did."

The Bodyguard
The smash-hit box-office success of Christmas 1992, *The Bodyguard* had the perfect combination of

> *"There are certain singers that occupy that territory that includes a world-class voice, real elegance and a physical presence. Diana Ross and Barbra Streisand are two. Whitney Houston is another."*
>
> *Kevin Costner*

glamour, action, suspense and romance. The result was a classic of the great Hollywood tradition: bigger than life, earth-shatteringly dramatic and full of variety. Larry Kasdan's original script was written in the early days of his career, with the late Steve McQueen in mind, but it wasn't until 1990 that Kevin Costner took it on and enlisted Mick Jackson (director of Steve Martin's modern comedy of manners, *LA Story*) to work with him. But the biggest problem was finding a co-star.

"Do you choose an actress and teach her to sing?" pondered Jackson. "Or do you choose a singer and hope that you can find an acting ability there? That seemed to be the better and, it

Bobby Brown guested on stage at several of his wife's concerts in 1993.

turned out, wiser option. She's great." Costner convinced Whitney not to take acting lessons, and the two stars spent many hours working together to make her character come to life. Whitney's stylistic approach was a simple one—to treat her script the way she treats her music, and let it flow from the heart. "It's easy for me to stand on stage and sing and relate to people," she said. "I feel the beats to music. I know when to become powerful and when to quiet it down. That was the hardest part in acting—learning the words and letting them flow like I was singing."

The screen was made for Whitney
The singer's movie début could hardly have been more of a success, and her worries about failing as an actress were soon dispelled by the public's reaction. They flocked to *The Bodyguard* in their millions. The movie premièred in November, taking $27 million (£18 million) in its first week. By the end of 1992 it had scored a massive $200 million (£135 million) worldwide. Following its UK release on Boxing Day 1992, the film rocketed to the Number 1 position to become one of the top five earners in UK box office history, taking £17 million ($25 million). And when

Rachel and Frank dance to 'I Will Always Love You' on their first date.

The immaculately dressed Bobby Brown and Whitney Houston, the ultimate showbiz couple.

it was released on video in the UK in March 1993, more than two million people rented the film in the first seven days, accounting for a full 20 per cent of *all* home video rentals that week.

The music of The Bodyguard

The album of the movie features six new Whitney Houston tracks, five of which have been released as singles in their own right, including the outrageously successful 'I Will Always Love You'. On its release in November 1992 it immediately broke the US record for the most albums sold in one week. By the end of the year it was selling almost a million copies a week in the USA alone, making it the third best-selling album of the year after only five weeks!

It went on to sell more than ten million copies in the USA alone, and 22 million worldwide—the second most successful soundtrack album ever, after *Saturday Night Fever*. It has already sold more copies than the Pink Floyd LP *Dark Side of the Moon*, which spent an unbroken 736 weeks on the album chart. The album also featured 'I Have Nothing', written by David Foster and Linda Thompson, which was reputedly inspired by the themes to early James Bond movies.

'I Have Nothing' became the sixth best-selling single of 1993 in the US, reached Number 3 in the British charts, and was nominated for an

Heartbreaker Costner with record-breaking Houston in a romantic movie—the combination couldn't fail to produce a Number 1 album.

Academy Award for Best Song. More hit singles followed: a cover version of the familiar Chaka Khan track 'I'm Every Woman' produced by long-time collaborator Narada Michael Walden; 'Run To You', in which Rachel Marron features in a stunning video, swathed in diaphanous white veils; and 'Queen Of The Night', a raunchy,

> *"It never did that well for me. It did well for you because you put all that stuff into it."*
>
> *Dolly Parton*

guitar-heavy rock-dance groove, which was co-written by Whitney herself and introduces a fusion of new colours in her musical palette.

'I Will Always Love You'

"This is kinda a cowboy song, huh?" says Rachel Marron as she dances with her date for the evening. "I mean, it's so depressing. Have you listened to the words?"

"It is kinda depressing," replies Frank Farmer. "It's one o' those somebody's-always-leaving-somebody songs."

There is surely no doubt that the success of *The Bodyguard* and its soundtrack album revolved

Left: Bobby Brown, clutching daughter Bobbi, born March 1993.

Right: Shielded from the spotlight—Whitney with daughter Bobbi Kristina, leaving Radio City Music Hall in New York after a performance.

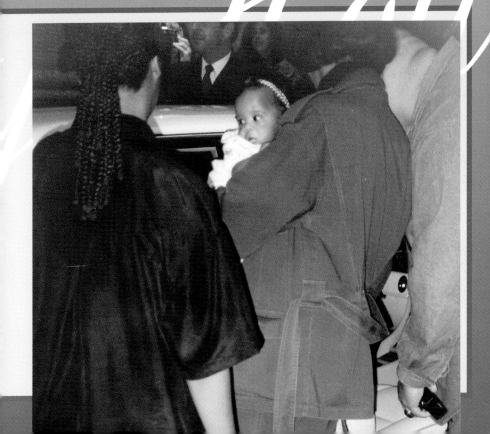

around one, wonderful song. Written by country and western star Dolly Parton, and first recorded in 1974, 'I Will Always Love You' is unforgettable. The song was a minor hit for Dolly in 1982 when it was included in the soundtrack of her movie *The Best Little Whorehouse In Texas*, but with Whitney's vocal the melody really becomes magical. "It never did that well for me," Dolly Parton told Whitney. "It did well for you because you put all that *stuff* into it."

Released as a single in November, Whitney's tenth US chart-topper became the best-selling single of 1992 in the UK and USA, spending 10 weeks and 14 weeks respectively at the Number 1 position. In America it sold 4 million copies in 1992, but still managed to achieve the Number 3 place in the best-selling singles of 1993! 'I Will Always Love You' is one of the ten best-selling singles of all time in the USA, and the third most successful UK single in terms of chart success (highest number of weeks in the highest position). The song even made headlines in the UK when a young

The stunning 1993 sell-out world tour.

woman was successfully prosecuted by her next-door neighbour for playing the song over and over again at high volume, day and night!

'I Will Always Love You' holds the UK record for the most number of singles sold by a female solo artist (1,200,000), a title previously held by Jennifer Rush with 'The Power Of Love'. The CD single is officially the biggest international seller of all time. It was re-released in December 1993, to considerable renewed interest.

The crowds flock to hear that song

In March 1993 Whitney gave birth to a daughter, named Bobbi Kristina, but this didn't stop her setting off on a world tour, which reached Britain in November for dates at Sheffield Arena and London's Earls Court Stadium. Whitney was frequently joined on stage by her husband and baby, and at an exclusive after-show party at London's Hard Rock Café she was serenaded by a bespectacled Bobby in

Utterly relaxed in the Nineties—Whitney performs more naturally on stage than she did on her early tours.

> *"When I first started I was having a lot of fun. But it ain't fun no more. I enjoy what I do...but it's not fun."*
>
> *Whitney Houston*

front of her 150-strong entourage. Many of the audience members at the sell-out shows were new fans, and there was, of course, one song that they always wanted to hear. The climactic 'I Will Always Love You' put a chill in the air as Whitney's extraordinary voice boomed out over the heads of thousands of stunned, silent listeners—but as soon as the song came to its climax, the roar of the crowd was inevitably deafening. Not only has the song become a classic on CD, it is also one of the most spine-tingling concert show-stoppers of all time.

Always a beaming smile for the audience—and on the 1993 tour, Whitney had more reason than ever to smile.

Whitney finally has it all, but fame can be a heavy price to pay.

Just wanna be with my family

There are always rumours about Whitney's future (and a remake of *A Star is Born* may be on the cards). One project that she has always longed to work on is a full-length gospel album. "That pop dance stuff I can run off in my sleep; I feel like I'm a kid at an amusement park" she told UK's *The Sunday Times* in 1990, a little too frankly. "But gospel is very precious, intricate and delicate to me. You don't just sing it, you live it. There are a few steps I have to make before I'm ready for that. But it will happen. God knows that."

But despite this dream, the future holds only one real goal for Whitney now. Happiness. "You know what I feel?" she asked *Rolling Stone* in 1993. "I feel old. For the most part, since I was 11 years old, I've been working. I did the nightclubs, I did the modeling, all that stuff...When I first started I was having a lot of fun. But it ain't fun no more. I enjoy what I do...but it's not fun." For now, Whitney's idea of fun is being with her baby and trying to live something close to a normal life: "Man, when I gave birth to her and when they put her in my arms, I thought 'This has got to be it. This is the ultimate.' I haven't experienced anything greater."

Chronology

1963   Whitney Houston born in Newark, New Jersey, USA on August 9.

1974   First appearance as a solo vocalist, at New Hope Baptist Church, where her mother is Minister of Music.

1983   Spotted by Clive Davis at a showcase arranged by Arista A&R executive Gerry Griffith, she is immediately signed up. Davis begins to groom her for stardom.

1984   Appears on minor hit records 'Hold Me' with Teddy Pendergrass and 'Take Good Care Of My Heart' with Jermaine Jackson, while work on her first album continues. Davis enlists top names to assure a dazzling début.

1985   Début album *Whitney Houston* released. Single 'You Give Good Love' makes US Number 3, setting Whitney on the path to fame.

Two months after its release, 'Saving All My Love For You', written by Gerry Goffin and Michael Masser, hits US Number 1 and is consequently released in the UK, making Number 1 in December.

1986   In the States two more Number 1 hits follow—'How Will I Know' and 'The Greatest Love Of All'. She wins her first Grammy and her first Emmy before her 23rd birthday, and then sets off for her first world tour.

1987   More US Number 1 singles: 'I Wanna Dance With Somebody (Who Loves Me)' and 'Didn't We Almost Have It All', both from her second album *Whitney* (the first album by a solo female artist ever to enter the Billboard chart at Number 1).

1988   'Where Do Broken Hearts Go' and 'So Emotional' give her seven consecutive chart-toppers (the longest winning streak in chart history). Another world tour is crowned by an acclaimed appearance at Wembley Stadium in London, for the Nelson Mandela Birthday Concert.

1990 Sales of third album, *I'm Your Baby Tonight*, are disappointing (eventually reaching about seven million world-wide) despite spawning two Number 1 singles in the US (the title track and 'All The Man That I Need').

1991 Whitney is at the centre of rising nationalism as she releases single version of 'The Star-Spangled Banner'. World tour kicks off with controversial "Welcome Home Heroes" gig for Gulf War veterans, enhancing her public image as a "Lady Liberty" for the Nineties.

1992 Marries hip-hop star Bobby Brown (formerly of teen group New Edition) while pregnant with their first child. The release of her first film *The Bodyguard* (co-starring Kevin Costner) coincides with a soundtrack album featuring six new tracks, including smash hit 'I Will Always Love You'.

1993 Gives birth to a daughter, Bobbi Kristina, in March. Four more hit singles are culled from The Bodyguard, including 'Queen Of The Night', the first release of a song co-written by the star herself. Despite public admissions of dissatisfaction with her career, a sell-out world tour leaves audiences breathless.

1994 Release of the first Bobby Brown/Whitney Houston collaboration single, 'Something In Common'. Whitney wins 8 more American Music Awards, and Record of the Year (for 'I Will Always Love You)' and Best Female Vocal at the Grammy Awards.

Discography

ALBUMS

Whitney Houston
February 1985
UK: Arista 610359
US: Arista ARCD-8212
Charts: UK 2, US 1

Whitney
May 1987
UK: Arista 258141
US: Arista ARCD-8405
Charts: UK 1, US 1

I'm Your Baby Tonight
November 1990
UK: Arista 261039
US: Arista ARCD-8616
Charts: UK 6, US 3

The Bodyguard
November 1992
UK: Arista 07822 186992
US: Arista 18699
Charts: UK 1, US 1

Albums featuring Whitney Houston:

Dynamite
(Jermaine Jackson)
June 1984
UK:Arista 610150
Charts: UK 7, US 19

Love Language
(Teddy Pendergrass)
July 1986
UK: Asylum 960317-2
US: Elektra 60317-2
Charts: UK –, US 38

Very Special Christmas
(Various artists)
November 1987
(US release only)
US: A&M CD-3911
Charts: US 20

Heaven
(BeBe & CeCe Winans)
March 1989
US: Capitol C2-90959-2
Charts: UK–, US 95

One Moment In Time
(Various artists)
September 1988
UK: Arista 259299
US:Arista ARCD-8551
Charts: UK-, US 31

Through The Storm
(Aretha Franklin)
May 1989
UK:Arista 259842
US: Arista 8572
Charts: UK 41, US 16

Bobby
(Bobby Brown)
September 1992
UK: MCA MCD-10695
US:MCA MCASD-10417
Charts: UK 11, US 2

SINGLES

Someone For Me
April 1985
Charts: UK–

You Give Good Love
July 1985
Charts: UK–, US 3

Saving All My Love For You
October 1985
Charts: UK 1, US 1

How Will I Know
January 1986
Charts: UK 5, US 1

The Greatest Love Of All
March 1986
Charts: UK 8, US 1

I Wanna Dance With Somebody (Who Loves Me)
May 1987
Charts: UK 1, US 1

Didn't We Almost Have It All

August 1987
Charts: UK 14, US 1

So Emotional
November 1987
Charts: UK 5, US 1

Where Do Broken Hearts Go
February 1988
Charts: UK 14, US 1

Love Will Save The Day
May 1988
Charts: UK 10, 9

One Moment In Time
September 1988
Charts: UK 1, US 5

It Isn't, It Wasn't, It Ain't Never Gonna Be (with Aretha Franklin)
August 1989
Charts: UK 29, US 41

I'm Your Baby Tonight
October 1990
Charts: UK 5, US 1

All The Man That I Need

December 1990
Charts: UK 13, US 1

The Star-Spangled Banner
March 1991
Charts: US 20

Miracle
April 1991
(US release only)
Charts: US 9

My Name Is Not Susan
July 1991
Charts: UK 29, US 20

I Belong To You
September 1991
(UK release only)
Charts: UK 54

I Will Always Love You
November 1992
Charts: UK 1, US 1

I'm Every Woman
February 1993
Charts: UK 4, US 4

I Have Nothing
April 1993

Charts: UK 3, US 4

Run To You
June 1993
Charts: UK 15, US 31

Queen Of The Night
November 1993
(UK release only)
Charts: UK 14

I Will Always Love You
December 1993
(UK re-release only)
Charts: UK 25

Singles featuring Whitney Houston:

Hold Me (Teddy Pendergrass)
June 1984
(UK release Jan 86)
Charts: UK 44, US 44

Something In Common (Bobby Brown)
January 1994
(UK release only)
Charts: UK 16

Index

(Italics refer to illustrations)

Picture Acknowledgements

Photographs reproduced by kind permission of **London Features International**; **Pictorial Press** /Brett Lee, /Mayer, /Rudi Reiner, /Giovanny Romero, /Gene Shaw, /David Seelig, /Warner Brothers, /Vinnie Zuffante; **Redferns** /Suzi Gibbons, /Bob King, /FL Lange, /Ebet Roberts; **Relay Photos** /André Csillag.
Front cover picture: **London Features International**